Read the Fine Print Before You Say *"I Do"*

D1548732

by

Jack Leipert

PAULIST PRESS
New York/Mahwah, N.J.

Library of Congress Cataloging-in-Publication Data

Leipert, Jack.
    Read the fine print before you say "I do" / Jack Leipert.
        p.   cm.
    ISBN 0-8091-3464-0 (pbk.)
    1. Marriage–Religious aspects–Catholic Church. 2. Marriage
Counseling. I. Title
BX2250.L3885   1994
248.8′44–dc20   94-5156
                                                              CIP

Published by Paulist Press
997 Macarthur Boulevard
Mahwah, NJ 07430

Printed and bound in the
United States of America

Contents

Preface

This book needs writing as much as it needs reading. Doing therapy and counseling with couples as a clinical social worker has fine-tuned my listening skills and made me solution-oriented. Giving retreats for married people and offering family "missions" throughout the United States has wised me up to the joys, sorrows, and glories of this sacrament called marriage. My many years as priest and pastor have allowed me to be an intimate companion to hundreds of couples at every stage of their relationship.

The people I will introduce to you are real, their names fictitious, but their situations familiar in every parish. I might be talking about your marriage. If not now, then later.

I've often wondered why we don't have some easy-to-read, practical and pastoral book on marriage topics available for engaged couples in our parishes. With divorce a shattering and all too common reality for so many of our people, why not offer some reflections on grace at work in the struggles of married men and women to hang-in there, when the world says "quit."

This book offers hope. I've taken what I've learned from couples about their pitfalls, temptations and successes, and offer it as food for thought to all married people. As you see yourselves on the menu, you will taste the possibilities for growth in every crisis, and be satisfied that you said to your mate, "I will love you in good days and bad, in sickness and health, for richer or poorer, till death do us part."

1

Getting to Know One Another

I don't hear an argument anymore. When I welcome the young couples who come to discuss a wedding date with me, they know I mean it when I say they are radicals. With such a high rate of divorce, with so many of their friends already on the casualty list, I applaud them for their courage. To say, "I love you forever," is to be counted among the few and brave today.

Yet, they are scared when they see me. Politely, they remark how much they enjoy the mass since I came. Like most young people, they have taken a temporary "leave of absence" from church attendance. They feel awkward about this and wonder how I will judge them. My verdict: they've taken a bold step in the right direction.

I enjoy young people in their twenties, so I am concerned that they draw upon the riches of their Catholic heritage and know that we as church are rooting for them to make it.

The couples I see seem to be a little older these days, but many still meet in bars as in yesteryear. A good number yearned for each other in high school (from a safe distance), then, one day, said "hello" at last, overcame their shyness and began their belated romance. I get a sizable group of "kiss-and-make-up-ers," who have an endless series of near-brawls before they get friendly long enough to talk marriage. And it happens more and

3

more that one of the pair has a child. Then courtship gets more complicated.

During those first minutes of the interview, we are all checking each other out. It doesn't take long for me to develop a fondness for the couple—maybe it's my father instinct. Then I make my solemn pronouncement. I don't get more serious in tone or body language than this:

> By getting married in the Catholic Church, you are making *three* statements: First, that you love each other for keeps; second, that this love will somehow be rooted in Jesus Christ and his value system; third, at least one of you will find a primary support system and family in the Catholic Church.

Then they look at me like they've been hit with something profound. Until then, the details of renting the hall, whom to invite, what to wear, and where to honeymoon—the wedding is what mattered. When the idea that this is sacred stuff they're dealing with hits them (and it usually occurs at just about this time), I sense a newfound respect developing between us.

Later, I will discuss more fully the Christian and Catholic dimension as they unfold in the relationship.

"Tell me what you have going for you to make this relationship work? and don't use the word 'love'."

"Friendship," she says.

"Good communication," he jumps in.

Because I do hear those two responses regularly now, I figure some "in" words from Oprah Winfrey and Phil Donahue have turned them on.

Since they are friends and can talk about anything, we explore and examine areas in a relationship that are key in getting to know each other.

I Can Change You

Nancy was so sure that her even temper would calm Bill once they were married. Sure, he would rant and rave occasionally, slam his fist into the wall after a heated squabble, and, oh yes, once did shove her "just a little." She could quiet him on dates and slowly ease him into equilibrium. And, besides, there was that other side of him, generous to a fault. It was a trade-off she could live with, and she was confident that he would "shape up."

The shape of things worsened once they were married. Verbal and physical abuse escalated until the police and, later, the lawyers got involved. Nancy was the one who changed: from a calm port in a storm to a capsized dinghy.

I cringe when I think of the mistake I made with John and Kate. I was a young priest, unfamiliar with the dynamics of addiction. Here was another case of "change would come later." John discussed his drinking openly in our pre-marriage interviews. He had some "wild times." Who didn't? I thought. But he would be a good provider. At the time, he had a spotless work record and a promised promotion in sight. Kate was happy with his ambition, but more than a little nervous about his "social drinking." It was she who brought it up in the discussion, not me. I brushed it off as "sowing wild oats," and reassured them both that marriage routine and responsibility and, later, children would not give John time to indulge. What poor advice! How we distorted a painful reality that begged to be addressed at the beginning of a relationship, not in a detox ward of a hospital two years later, after a drunk-driving accident.

Sure, we can influence, challenge and root for each other, but nobody can change another. Those who enter a marriage believing this myth pay a heavy price later. All engaged couples would be wise to check for bad habits during the dating game. I always ask, "Are you worried about drinking, drugs, gambling, temper tantrums, overeating, jealousy, smoking?" . . . whatever.

What Do You Do for Fun

Recently, I've witnessed a budding romance between a couple who met at a "hospitality house." Now the purpose of this facility is to provide temporary boarding and meals for family members while their loved ones remain in critical condition at a nearby Catholic hospital. Donna and Glenn got room and board and a tiny stipend for offering several hours of service in this inner-city home. They started as partners, grew to become friends, and eventually fell in love.

When asked what sparked their interest in the other, they both replied, "The way he/she had fun." Unconsciously, they observed each other enjoy people, enjoy simple things, laugh while they washed dishes, tease a shy child, hold a grandmother's hand. They saw quality in each other, real class. And they really had fun together!

On the other end of the continuum, at another parish I pastored, the hot spot for singles (the "meat market" they called it) was the college bar. There, in the midst of loud noises and flashing strobe lights, uninhibited after a few drinks, young people sized each other up. If they liked what they saw, they went home with it, or, at least, got a phone number scribbled on a napkin for future reference. I worry about such meetings. Not just because of AIDS, but because of the way fun is defined in such places.

I tell couples—they laugh—to look for prospective

dates by checking out the folks who help at Special Olympics, serve as Big Brothers and Sisters, volunteer at parish events, are involved in community projects and (I get an extra chuckle here) can be spotted enjoying an occasional afternoon reading in the library.

Fun is good medicine at every stage of married life. I salute and recommend the kind of fun that costs little and demands the most interaction. For so many couples a movie is considered a night out.

If your future spouse does not know how to have fun in creative, informal, spontaneous, non-sexual, non-expensive ways—ways that build a relationship—expect a couch potato, sipping suds, waiting for life to entertain him or her when you're married. Doesn't sound like fun to me!

Can You Really Talk to Each Other?

We all know that ice-cream tastes better when you're in love, music is livelier, and time can stand still. But how is your conversation? My clinical and pastoral experience teaches me that couples, in general, never mastered the skill of clear communication. They talk when they should listen, and listen when they should talk. And when they talk, they don't do it with both ears. When they fight, they don't fight fair; someone always walks away a loser. There is a better way and it can be learned while dating; ideally, it should be taught in high school. In my parish we insist on an afternoon workshop devoted to good communication skills.

When Joyce got angry, she pouted. Sometimes she stewed so long she developed physical symptoms. She couldn't tell Tony what she liked and dared not tell him what she didn't like.

"She just tenses up and gives me that icy stare."

Did he ask her what was wrong?

"Yes, but she just says if you love me you should know."

How did he deal with this cold treatment?

"I called her names, accused her of really wanting 'out' of the relationship."

Both Tony and Joyce needed some education quickly. This way of non-communication will surface as a pattern in marriage if not nipped in the bud early.

Joyce and Tony needed to use "I" messages and describe feelings in a non-judgmental way.

"I feel lonely and insecure when you don't call during the day, Tony," goes over much better than, "You don't care for me, you bum!" God has commissioned couples to become *active* listeners. Nothing gifts a person more than being understood.

Yes, indeed, assertiveness and active listening must be skills every parish offers couples during their preparation time. If we are in the business of preventive medicine, the parish is the place to offer a course, a class, or seminar...*something* on how to fight fair.

Good communication is learning a new language and probably unlearning bad habits. Investment of time, energy and even money in this area will pay dividends a hundredfold.

What a wedding gift to offer a couple: A communication workshop on *you*!

Where Does Faith Fit In?

In getting to know each other, it would be a grave mistake not to explore the faith dimension or lack of it in courtship. As important as communication, budgeting, parenting and all the other topics I will address in this little book are, the most important and, sadly, least significant to couples is discussing the practice of faith. Here is an all too familiar scenario.

Meg is a cradle Catholic. She received all the sacraments and had rudimentary catechesis. She couldn't imagine being anything else but Catholic. She attends mass with regularity, but her piety has little impact on her day-to-day decisions. She has no Christian support group, does not feel comfortable using the Bible for private devotions, and could never imagine praying together with her male friend on a date. Matt loves Meg but is concerned with her lack of depth and passion as a Christian. He attends mass with her but never gets a good answer about the countless questions he has regarding Catholic belief and practice. You see, Matt is a convinced Christian, an ardent reader of the Bible, and belongs to a men's Christian fellowship group.

They enjoy so many dimensions of their relationship together, but Matt's strident faith bubbles while Meg's has the sound of a dull thud. Conflict is inevitable when love fever wears off. Like many pastors, I am vitally concerned about the thousands of unconverted and unformed Catholic youth. I want to see our parishes develop a vibrant formation process for the many unevangelized young adults who, in my experience, are hungry for spiritual mentors at this teachable moment.

I find that most have no concept of the word "grace"; they are pleasantly surprised to hear that God places solutions in their lives to *stay* married. To hear that vows empower them, don't bridle them, frees them to hear commitment as not another dirty word. With the many distorted notions of love conveyed by the media and pop psychology, the word "covenant" carries the hope of their not being another divorce statistic. I want men and women getting to know each other to learn the meaning and message of these Christian words.

Couples need to ask each other, "What does your faith mean to you?" since key values about money, family, work, friendship, sex, illness, conflict and all the choices that matter hinge on the question Jesus still asks of us: "Who do *you* say that I am?"

What Will You Do as a Last Resort

Always end the friendly pastoral visit with the crucial question, "When all else fails and the marital bubble bursts, then what will you do?"

In the getting-to-know-each-other stage couples seldom, if ever, discuss what to do with the last straw before it breaks their back.

"Suppose Jake won't communicate, no matter how much pleading you do, Rose?"

"I'll wait it out."

"What if the waiting wears thin?"

"I'll issue an ultimatum!"

And if Jake still won't bend?"

"I'll pray."

"And if prayer doesn't do it?"

"We'll divorce, of course!!"

I wish that couples would make a prenuptial agreement to *always* seek professional counseling as a must *before* they do it the American way: *quit.* Going to a priest or sister or other pastoral person may help ease the symptoms. But they are *not* trained to do therapy and it frightens me to see couples in the hands of a well-meaning incompetent. (Talk with people who have been given simplistic solutions to complex problems by pastors!) By all means, seek out a therapist with Christian principles and, if they have any bias, may it be in helping to salvage and revive the marriage—if humanly possible.

DISCUSSION QUESTIONS

1. What aspects of my life do I intend to change after marriage. Why?

2. What aspects of my life would I *not* be willing to change after marriage. Why?

2

Dealing with Families: Who Picks Up the Socks?

The last chapter dealt with important questions to be asked when getting to know each other. I would also suggest developing a sharp eye during family visits. Play detective; look for clues. Be sure to be discreet. Drop in on the homestead and prepare yourself for surprises.

It's no secret that lovers put their best foot forward in those early stages of courtship. Shocker! Bad habits at home, camouflaged by romance, surface soon enough in marriage.

Katie bathed in the little signs of affection, i.e., flowers, poems, cards, opened car doors, that Randy lavished on her. She took my dare and dropped by, unannounced, at Randy's home at various times for a period of a month. She snooped around enough to see socks and underwear hanging on door knobs that his mom would pick up—eventually. She observed that Randy assisted little in family chores and, when finally coerced, bellowed that much of this was "women's work" anyway. She had a good sneak preview of a drama that might be played out with her, once his best foot forward got in the door.

Nathan, on the other hand, discovered on his home visitation that his darling was also "Daddy's little girl." Pampered and protected all her life, Virginia looked to Nathan for Dad's same strong, protective arms. What, at first, stroked his ego, he later interpreted to be dependency. He broke off the relationship when it became painfully apparent he had a child on his hands, not a partner.

Family therapists find that we tend to gravitate to what we know, and unconsciously pick a future mate with an uncanny resemblance to a parent.

As Christians we do not believe that our lives are completely "predetermined"; with insight, we can throw cold water on our faces and make more rational choices of life companions.

Looking for Strengths

I was madly in love with Donna Reed: the woman who kept the kids and the house immaculate and still treated her husband like royalty when he returned home from the office. When I saw Donna Reed, Lucy, the Nelsons, the Waltons, and other idealized nuclear families on television, I figured we'd all turn out that way.

I see a different picture in our parishes. In my religious education program, forty percent of the kids are raised in single-parent homes and have different last names from their brothers and sisters.

Just when couples thought they could relax and sail more freely, since the kids were raised and gone from the nest—the kids suddenly come home again to roost. As our population of the aging grows, families are being forced into the strain of double-duty caretaking: grandparents and kids.

Out of this evolving network of people who share their lives together: the nuclear family (Mom and Dad); the single parent (by divorce and by choice); the blended family (step-children all together under the same roof); out of these havens of love and refuge come our candidates for the sacrament of marriage today. We must take these couples from their respective starting points and draw out their strengths.

Lily and Clark described their family of origin to me in what has become popular jargon: dysfunctional families. In reality, there is a wide spectrum of the normal, average, and healthy in every family tree. Lily's parents divorced when she was fifteen. Living with her mother who had to work outside the home to make ends meet, Lily assumed a major role in the raising of her siblings. When I inquired how she would use this *asset*, she look puzzled.

"True, you missed out on some quality time as a teenager, but you seem to be strong because of it."

"You mean my lack of social life as a teen will be a strength for my marriage?"

"Lily, damage was done, no doubt. But we both agree not enough to repress you or inhibit you. Clark knows you are capable of intimacy. If not, I'd be the first to send you for professional treatment before you'd walk down the aisle. Your family experience has taught you self-reliance, confidence and instilled a caring attitude. A good marriage needs those qualities in both parties."

Before my clinical training, before eighteen years of pastoral work, marriage and family retreats around the country, I was a romantic optimist; now I'm a realistic optimist. Everybody is flawed, handicapped, "dysfunctional" to some degree; isn't that the definition of original sin? Although I cautioned in the early part of this chapter against blind love, I also caution against giving oneself or anybody else a *label*. If your family origin hurt you and it doesn't require extensive therapy to repair the damage, then make lemonade out of the lemons life dealt you. You are not responsible for all the environmental and genetic variables that formed you, but God requires a creative response in how you deal the cards given. I tell this to every couple who harp too much on their family of origin's mistakes.

Playing Those Old Tapes

"If the man cheats, it's the woman's fault for not keeping him happy."
"Always kiss and make up before you go to bed."
"Never talk about religion or politics."
"A woman's place is at home".
"Use sex or the lack of it to make your point."
"Do *everything* as a family."
"The family that prays together, stays together."

Any of these tapes sound familiar? Do you agree with all of them? What are some of your own? We all carry in our conscious or unconscious minds assumptions, values, beliefs and philosophies inherited from our families that need to be examined and challenged before couples build their love nests. Some of these tapes are good and practical and might well be kept on the recorder; others are half-truths or glaring distortions that come out sooner or later in marriage.

Brett battled pounding headaches and high blood pressure for most of his ten years married to Wanda. His extreme irritability baffled his wife and all who knew her to be patient and affirming. With counseling and spiritual direction, he was able to surface a tape that played incessantly: "You must be successful in all you do." Never mind that he held a good job and did well at it; he wasn't at the top yet. Never mind that he coached the neighborhood kids as well as his own in little league; they never got a trophy. Never mind that he was an active member on his parish finance committee; he was never voted Parish Council President. Never mind that he provided well for Wanda and the kids; he never bought that dream house he promised her. Always seeking the prize and never enjoying the race took its toll on Brett in physical symptoms and spiritual unrest. Uncovering the message his own father drilled into his head as a child, he could debate it, confront it with a better message like, "enough is enough" and discard it as bunk. When he did this, the symptoms vanished and the marriage rebounded.

Corita loved her husband Mitch with a passion, yet she couldn't be passionate with him. On a scale of ten, Corita's sex drive was a *two* while Mitch was *ten* and over. Again, after counseling and spiritual direction, Corita surfaced the tape her mother gave: "Sex is a duty, never to be enjoyed." In its place she told herself, until she believed it: "Sex is God's gift to married people; it's an equal opportunity benefit."

Faulty tapes, learned in the family of origin, will play their lyrics and background music for couples who can't recognize the root of the noise and upheaval in their relationship.

How the Family Can Help

In conducting an Engaged Workshop recently, I asked the question, "What's your biggest worry in light of your upcoming wedding?" The answer amused and surprised me: "Which family to go to on holidays," was the common concern.

I was also touched, as were the engaged couples, by a parent on one of the panels, who wanted these young people to know that it is hard for a parent to stay uninvolved in such an important step for their child. It is natural to want to protect, to advise, to meddle a little.

Let me suggest some ways family members might intervene in unexpected and productive ways. First, in a non-lecturing fashion, share some of your mistakes. Did you not reserve enough quality time for yourselves while the kids were growing up? Tell them. Did you budget properly and set priorities. Tell them. Did you talk too much *at* each other and not listen enough? Tell them. Did you fail to affirm each other enough? Tell them. How did *your* in-laws affect you for good or bad. Tell them. What role did faith play in strengthening or alienating you? And by all means, if you believe in marriage, share that gladly. And, if you survived divorce, share the wisdom from your pain, without blaming your ex. All of these admissions will take courage. But if done in a non-threatening, sincere way, you've gifted them. If done in the right atmosphere, in the right tone, you might even leave them speechless.

And while you're in the gift-giving mode, *spend* some of your hard-earned money on them. I'm not talking about the hall, the band, or the shower. I've never once heard of parents paying for an Engaged Encounter Weekend (which just about every diocese offers) for their son or daughter. The price is cheap and the benefits long-lasting. Try it. You'll send a message that the *marriage* matters in a consumer culture that couldn't care less.

Then, let go.

That can be the hard part because they really haven't a clue to where those vows will lead them. There will be pain and sorrow, disillusionment and frustration, passion and boredom ahead for them. You know that, if you've worked at marriage for a while. Now you can't wipe their noses. Your joy will come as you see new life flow from that surrender.

DISCUSSION QUESTIONS

1. How do I define the role of wife?
   How do I define the role of husband?

2. How is this role similar to the example set by my parents? How is it different?

3. In what ways will we find support from our extended families?

4. In what ways will it be necessary that we become independent from our extended families?

3

Facing Sexuality in Marriage— and Before

My voice, changing as it was, at age thirteen, strained even higher as I entered the booth to confess my secret sin to Fr. Dempsey. With my sensuous imagination, I entertained impure thoughts while browsing through Home and Garden magazine. My pastor was notoriously irate over sexual sins; severe penances always accompanied a good tongue-lashing. So, timidly, I leaned against the screen in that dark box and squeaked my transgression. To my astonishment, the old priest tenderly addressed me: "As you become a young woman, changes will take place in your body...."

We've come a long way from those scrupulous days when people lined up for hours, sometimes on a weekly basis, to seek absolution for dirty thoughts, desires and touches (with ourself or others)—and the number of times needed counting, too.

Now, there is emphasis on sins against justice and sins of omission. If we get a few young people to go to Reconciliation to confess these social sins, we congratulate ourselves on our preaching. Considering our world scene, this seems a better direction.

But, considering our world situation in the light of sexual abuse, AIDS, abortion, pornography and the cheapening of sex by the media, why are pastoral leaders

19

reluctant to preach even one homily a year about sexual sin?

Perhaps we lose courage because of the sexual scandals that have plagued the priesthood in recent years. Maybe we've lost nerve because of the breakdown of the family unit, or perhaps the high divorce rate, or the climbing Catholic illiteracy and relativism just overwhelms the used-to-be fire and brimstone preacher. Or could it be that a positive approach to chastity can't be found compelling enough to encourage abstinence and discipline?

Whatever the case, so many young people do not receive clear, consistent and objective guidance on the parish level in matters of *sexual morality*. The direction they receive comes in a mixed package from the world: Just say "no" because you don't want to catch AIDS or other venereal diseases, but *do* get overheated by all the steamy sex you want in the movies and television.

I want to offer some scenarios from my pastoral work, considering again the church's traditional teaching regarding premarital sex.

Is It Love or Loneliness?

Kristin, my best lector, came into the sacristy to take a final look at the readings before mass. I welcomed her bouncy, friendly "hello" and looked forward to our usual round of teasing. This time she was different; she looked sullen and distraught.

"No jokes today, Kristin?"

"No, Father, the joke is over," she said with a grim finality in her voice.

"Tell me what's going on," I encouraged.

"Dale and I broke up. He said the relationship was getting too sticky, I was too possessive. I don't understand. He was my life. I shared everything with him. Before meeting him, my days were so ordinary. We even had sex because I believed he completed me in every way. Now I feel empty and so *lonely*." Kristin has lots of company in the lonely hearts club. She, like many women "who love too much," will confuse sexual union with intimacy. And, unfortunately, plenty of men are still around who play on that vulnerability. In recent years, I have seen the tables turned more often, with men also as victims of love hunger.

It can't be emphasized strongly enough that standing on one's own two feet, with a healthy dose of self-acceptance, is the best ad for a prospective mate.

At least Irene and Don felt that way. They were a couple who gave me a bit of wisdom that every lover might check out: *How comfortable are you with solitude?*

According to Irene, "When I can go for long walks alone and enjoy my own company, make a quiet, directed retreat and not get fidgety, even keep a personal diary where I treasure *my thoughts and feelings, then* I can love Don from inner strength not weakness."

Don claims, "Sure, there are times when sex is a 'quick fix' for me; *then* I'm grabbing for something, not sharing. When I take care of myself, enrich my life with quiet music, good books and healthy friendships with other men and women, I approach my wife, not out of lust, but *desire*." After twenty years of marriage, this couple argues that the desperate search for sex on the part of many couples is a result of a fear of solitude. In fear of being alone, they use sex as an antidote, and end up lonely.

Discipline Now; Dividends Later

Admittedly, couples who take seriously the church's teaching about abstinence and discipline before marriage are not carrying banners yet, but they make a good case. As often as possible, I get these folks to visit with engaged people and share their convictions. Here is a sample of the comments they make:

"It's not that I didn't want to have sex," says Paul. "At times I felt that three cold showers a day were needed to do the trick. Sylvia valued sex as a gift from each other for the wedding night. I did, too, although I wouldn't let on to my buddies. We needed to practice discipline *together*, and the closer the wedding day, the tougher it got."

So what did their "discipline" look like?

"Discipline is not just will power and saying 'no.' For us it meant using strategies," reported Sylvia. "The first thing needed is a *sense of humor*. When the place or the time was out-of-bounds, we knew we had to channel our energy into some silly project right away—to relieve tension. We made *rules* for ourselves way before passion had a chance to take over. We *talked out* the reasons for waiting: our faith, our priorities, a relationship built upon something stronger than sex." And the talking never stopped," added Paul. "We needed and gave constant reminders. Our acquaintances were quite sexually active, but their relationship didn't have the depth of ours. So we found friends who shared the same Christian values. We formed a sort of *support group*. That's what the church is supposed to offer anyway! Without it, the pressure to conform would've toppled our idealism."

Sylvia adds one last note, "When we slip, when we break our rules, when in weakness we disregard the gospel, we know enough to repent, to get to the *sacrament of reconciliation* and the *eucharist* regularly."

There's the ideal, then there's the real. When Marcus and Angie came to visit me they were badly shaken. They were pregnant, embarrassed and worried how their parents would accept them. But first they wanted to test my reaction. After being assured that I was with them and that I would offer my supportive presence as they told their parents, they could then pour out their fears: emotional, physical and financial. Fortunately, they were not going to marry under pressure, although they were tempted. They weren't going to abort the child, although there were moments of panic. They responsibly committed themselves to parenthood.

Our diocese has a strong support network through Catholic Family Services where trained counselors could assist this couple every step of the way. Referrals would be made to offer financial assistance with medical bills. A Mentor would be assigned this couple to guarantee that sound nutritional advice was given to the mother, and the step-by-step development of the fetus thoroughly explained. If tensions got too high at home, our diocese has support couples who would take Angie into their home at anytime during her pregnancy. This real concern for this couple's practical challenges took the terror out of their predicament.

Unplanned parenthood within a marriage can also be disconcerting. A couple may decide to wait to have a child until the relationship is more seasoned, the financial security on better footing, or the world looks brighter. Surprise! Junior makes his or her debut and the couple must discuss hard questions. How does the man feel about his wife working now? How does the woman feel about dividing her time between working and nurturing? Will the couple share the baby's wake-up calls, the diapering, the new chores? What are their feelings about day care? What about help from the extended family? Will grandparents or other blood relatives save the day? A couple would do well to discuss surprise packages to cushion the shock and avoid panic attacks later.

What About Sex and Sexuality Later?

What a sex education couples give me!

Couples with small children find sex a less frequent activity, sometimes, as they adjust to their sweetheart assuming mommy and daddy roles. If they are smart, they build in time for romance.

Vera and Scott take turns *surprising* each other. One week Vera schedules quality time—let's say dinner out at his favorite restaurant. The next week Scott may delight Vera with a shopping mall spree and a movie (thank God for grandma's baby-sitting service). Their sexual union becomes a celebration.

Middle-aged couples tell me about the great turnabout. He mellows out; she become more aggressive. Some men swear they feign a headache to ward off their wives' amorous overtures. While menopause can create problems, it can also give new freedom to women to enjoy sex more playfully. Men go through a sort of change-of-life, too. As they face their mortality, they can obsess about staying young and shun the wife who reminds them of the aging process; or they can take stock of the marriage, make changes based on reality and turn a potential crisis into an opportunity for growth.

Kent had to learn a lesson that many men are slow in grasping; love-making *starts* in the morning over coffee, *builds* during those little thoughtful exchanges during the day, and the grand *finale* is in bed—probably at night, although "lunch breaks" are prime times for some couples in my parish. His wife, Nan, enjoyed her new-found assertiveness.

"I now tell my husband what feels good and I've educated him to know the value of long embraces after sex. I insist that we talk before, during, and after lovemaking. He's become more patient; I've become more forward: a happy combination for both of us."

I know a couple married sixty-five years who keep a naughty twinkle in their eyes. They go on a major honeymoon every decade. They write poetry to each other and, although I'm too timid to ask them, rumor has it that they still turn each other on. Yes, a sex life can be alive and well into the twilight years, experts tell us.

Married people at all stages know the need for abstinence and discipline during illnesses and uncomfortable times during pregnancy. To live chastely before marriage can be a good rehearsal for tough times later.

Some Warning Signs

Sadly, I don't know many couples who have ever read Pope Paul VI's encyclical, "On Human Life." There is much that is beautiful in this letter. I worry when I see more and more couples excluding the possibility of new life from their sexuality. I'm not referring to abortion here. I'm talking about *ruling out* children as a part of marriage, considering them an inconvenience. The Hispanic notion of children as a "gift" is still Catholic teaching.

When couples use *sex as a weapon* to get even or manipulate, they sin, too. They sin mortally, deal a death blow to the marriage, when they give what is promised exclusively to their spouse to someone else. I have not seen many marriages rebuild trust successfully after *adultery,* although the grace of God, the sacrament of reconciliation, and good professional help can offer hope of healing.

Sex as Sacred

There is an old heresy that says if something feels good, it must be bad. Not so, according to scripture. Sex is the great gift given to people who covenant with God in marriage. It is a reward and encouragement for the sacrifices a couple make in loving each other in season and out-of-season, when they are open to life and when they promise faithfulness. "What God has joined together, let nobody separate."

DISCUSSION QUESTIONS

1. How will you build time for togetherness after your marriage?

2. Are there any conflicting values or stresses as we look at the meaning that sex has in our lives?

4

Children

We make a big deal of baptisms in my parish. Small enough to make baptism during mass personal, yet big enough to keep the folks curious about new faces, we make an impact on the new mom and dad. As they stand before the congregation, they state the name of their baby, and then answer one of the most important questions of their lives; will you accept the responsibility of raising your children in the faith by word and example? The godparents are then questioned about their support. I then challenge the congregation in this small town, to live in such a way that a child will want to become a part of the church–because *this* is where the action is. After the actual baptism, I carry the child down the aisle and introduce him or her to the "extended family." The parents get the message and so does the parish. I am emphatic about the difference it will make for a child to grow up in a Christian home, as opposed to having the classic Bunker Family (Archie and Edith). Instead of learning the word "nigger," the child will learn "brother" and "sister"; instead of the word "hate," the child will experience the word "love"; instead of "war," the child will know the word "peace."…. A child will grow to become radically different in such an atmosphere. One might even say out-of-step.

Time will tell if the parents keep their baptismal

promise. And their actions will surely speak louder than their words. When I served as pastor in an inner-city parish, I was inspired by a mother and six-year-old daughter passing sandwiches to poor people from our kitchen window. We had a volunteer system as a part of Christian Service, and this pair won the hearts of our daily guests with their courtesy and kindness. What a lesson in Christian love this child learned at the side of her mother!

I chuckle every Sunday when I see one large family occupy the same pew, all six boys' hands to their sides, blank stares, never moving their lips, *just like dad.* Children do imitate what they see!

I would estimate that forty percent of my parish kids in religious education classes don't attend mass on weekends. But there is a note of hope in all this. Often, kids shepherd the parents back to the fold by the questions they ask.

"Dad, why, if it's so special to receive Jesus in communion, don't you go every week?"

"Mom, the other kids go to Bible school. Will you take me?"

Once I challenged some second graders who had just made their first communion, "What can *you* do to get Mom and Dad to go to mass with you?

"Throw cold water on them."

"Tell Grandma."

"Ride my bike by myself to church."

These were some of the responses.

Though I worry about parents fulfilling their religious commitment, I know that parenting is tough. As a parish, we need to offer *parenting classes*, and sessions on *listening skills* for new parents, maybe as a part of preparation for baptism. Getting parent support groups going for parents with tots to teens wouldn't be a bad idea either. And during those teen years, let's offer training in *conflict resolution*. Every parish has resources to tap, and the local church is a non-threatening environment to provide such services. Talk to your pastoral leaders soon about such projects.

I see much verbal and physical abuse in the homes I visit. The stress level is high when parents are working two jobs, and especially when one can't find work at all. Children demand attention and patience from couples who often have little energy available. This is especially true when both parents must work outside the home.

Get Help

Marcie found herself spanking her two-year-old with an urge to really hurt the child.

"My nerves have had it after being cooped up with three little kids all day. It doesn't take much for me to yell at what used to be cute. My boy spills milk the second time in a row, he throws food, he messes his pants after I've just changed him. I need help!"

This is normal frustration; *before* it turns to action, contact Catholic Family Services or the nearest professional. Call a friend. Get the family to give you a break so you can get cooled down and get perspective.

Experts in child development claim those first five years are crucial in a child's having a good sense of self. A child must be able to *trust* at this stage; and if this trust is broken, the damage may be irreparable.

Quality Time

It is the presumption of this book that my words are addressed to a couple, engaged, or with their marriage still intact (a single parent is another issue requiring a strong support system).

Ralph and Bonny believed in oiling where it squeaked. They always attended to the child most in need at the moment, but their general approach was to treat their five kids as a happy little brood. Group activities, family games, even family rap sessions on a weekly basis built a tight-knit unit. But from time to time one of the children would pull antics at school and create havoc at home.

"We are a bonded family," Bonny protested to the counselor. "Why these outrageous acts at school and this resentment toward each other? After all, we do treat them all alike!"

"Maybe that's the problem," the therapists interjected. "Each one needs *quality time* with both parents *together* and each parent *separately*."

"That's impossible," blurted Ralph. "With our schedules, you're asking for too much!"

The counselor commended the couple for their efforts at keeping the cohesiveness of the family, yet pointed out some possibilities for *individual* attention built in through the week or month.

"How about a new ritual, a new rule: Each child has king or queen status for a day, an evening, an hour. During that time an activity of his or her choosing can be pursued with both mom and dad, or, more realistically, with one parent at a time."

Even if that might be hard rule to keep, little chores with a parent, like going to the grocery store together, working on the lawn together, washing the car together, might be golden opportunities to give each child the feeling of *uniqueness* that we all crave. This investment will pay dividends.

Other Family Dynamics

Not all acting out is due to wrangling for attention. According to Family Systems Theory, a child's self-defeating behavior could be his or her attempt to take on the illness of the whole family. In this case, no one person is the "identified culprit," but one child could develop symptoms to try to get the family in harmony.

At about the time Nathan's parents had openly discussed divorce, the school complaints about him deluged the family. He had always been an "A" student; now he was "C-." He didn't need to cheat; now he openly flaunted someone else's work as his own. What was the significance of this radical shift of behavior? It accomplished what he unconsciously wanted-it kept mom and dad involved with each other-as long as he was in trouble.

Or consider the case of young Marcia who developed severe asthmatic attacks. Her condition would be aggravated when her parents argued loudly. They learned to stifle their arguments to avoid upsetting their daughter. Her symptoms produced a temporary truce. Family members, most often the children, will do almost anything to keep the family in balance.

Boundaries

T.V. sitcom families model chaotic homes where teenagers call the shots and parents are wimps. Though teenagers rightly pursue their developmental task, *autonomy,* they clearly want boundaries. They are really as frightened of their developing bodies and volatile emotions as they are proud. They don't quite trust themselves and—in spite of themselves—they welcome a firm hand that says, "this far, no farther." Teenagers should never be used to fill the emotional void of a spouse. To be mom's "leaning shoulder" or dad's "little woman" presses a young person into inappropriate role expectations. They don't need "partners" or "buddies" as much as they need parents who set the parameters.

Clear Communication

"You can talk to me about anything," Darla's mom reassured her daughter. So, one day Darla broached the subject of condoms.

"Mom, I think I should carry some in my purse, you know, just in case. I know it's against my faith to have premarital sex, but I might get weak and then I don't want to be sorry."

"How can you talk about such a topic with me? It's disgusting! It's against all the values I taught you," screamed Darla's mom.

Mixed signals here? You bet. Certainly Darla needs direction but *first* she needs to be understood. After all, it was the parent who made the rule that no topic was taboo.

A better scenario might have gone like this... "Darla, you are concerned that you do the 'responsible' thing, in this case, the lesser of two evils. Your sexual urges scare you sometimes. Maybe we can look again at the *Christian perspective* on love and sex. It's what I believe in! Whichever decision you make, I'm glad you can talk things over with me."

Tell Them What They Do Right

At times allowing your child to feel the consequences of his or her actions, especially when they are painful, is the only route to go. We call that *tough love*. Parents don't understand the power of *positive reinforcement*! It is easier to dish out and accept, and more effective than negative reinforcement. The more *specific* and real we are in our praise, the better it works.

"Shannon, when you clean up after yourself at breakfast, I am grateful; I don't feel taken for granted," says his appreciative mom.

"Joe, when you get up and get ready for mass, I'm proud of you. I know you would love to sleep in on Sunday morning, but your even disposition that time of day gives a good example to your younger brothers." Such consistent affirmation of desired behavior builds affection and reduces resistance. We never hear enough about what we do right.

Have Fun with the Kids

I'm writing this at the time of the year when families have shed their winter clothes and are free of cabin fever. Parents are coaching or cheering at ball games and just letting their kids know they enjoy them.

I do get nervous when I see a father get uptight about his kid's less than perfect performance. When the competition is reasonable and the fun is plentiful, family bonding happens. And parents don't need to spend a lot of money, or give expensive gifts. Please, just be there for them!

One of the saddest phrases I hear as pastor is "if only":

"If only I played with my kids more."

"If only I said 'I love you' more often."

"If only I hugged my kid more."

"If only I just listened, not lectured."

"If only I could do it over again..."

Chances are good that if you've made the time to read

this book and want to put these suggestions into action *now*, you won't be an "if only" person.

Your children *are* God's gift to you. Enjoy!

DISCUSSION QUESTIONS

1. What goals will I have for my children?

2. Do we agree on these goals? How do we differ?

3. What will we have to do together to achieve these goals that we share?

4. How can we respectfully cooperate with each other when we do not agree in certain situations regarding our children?

5

Values and Money

Most priests, if they're honest with you, will tell you they dread wedding rehearsals. Not so with me. I enjoy kidding the nervous pair who at that point are at each other's throats. What causes so much tension—outside of if the ring-bearer will make it down the aisle—is the price tag for this gala affair. The church stipend is usually a pittance. But those gowns! That tux! That band! Those umpteen trinkets! Those invitations! That banquet! Those *bills*! Couples tell me love-spats start over money even before the wedding.

What Are Values?

Values are the relative worth, importance or utility you place on things. They are important statements about who you are, what you believe in, the stands you take, and the causes you herald. Values develop from childhood through early adulthood. Different cultures reflect different values.

Values influence all areas of life—moral, spiritual, aesthetic and economic. I want to focus on economic values because your approach to child raising, career decisions and how you treat your partner are shaped by these.

Learning about Your Money Values

The economic status you grew up with affects your values toward money. Some questions you might ask yourself:

How important was money in your family?
Did you have many material pleasures?
How did your family budget money?
Did you receive an allowance or earn your spending money?

Gayle grew up in a poor home with lots of love and hand-me-downs. His best friend, with a similar background, showed himself to be an entrepreneur at age ten with a yard-mowing business that earned good money. Gayle did not take his cue about finances from his parents who lived for the day; he imitated his best friend's drive and flair for the good life. By exploring your family's past and your development you can learn a great deal about yourself.

Learning About Your Partner's Money Values

Once you study your financial patterns, check out your future mate's:

Was your partner cut from the same mold, the same lifestyle?
How different or alike are your views on money?
Can you see potential conflict in the relationship over value differences?

One way to learn about each other's values is to compare approaches to child rearing. Will you want the same or better for your kids?

Dean insists that allowances are out. "Children need to contribute to the household without bribes," he maintains. He wants to see them get paper routes, or lawn jobs in grade school and tackle higher paying projects in high school. His fiance, Margo, sees childhood and adolescence as a time to focus on study and play. "I won't spoil the children. They will do their part around the house. A fair allowance will do the trick. I really don't want to see them become little capitalists."

Your values are not easily changed once they have been acquired. Values are at the core of your responsibility. Only with strong conviction and understanding can you change your values. In a relationship you will often have differing views about spending money. You cannot change your partner's values but, hopefully, you can compromise without loss of integrity.

Grace and Vic both valued security. Grace remembered how her family scraped to survive after her father's untimely death, leaving them with just enough insurance for the burial. She refused to see her children or herself in a similar predicament, so she wanted lots of money invested in a good insurance program. Vic, on the other hand, knew people who prospered with sound investments. He had a few rich uncles who would coach him in the stock market. They had three alternatives: 1) adopt the partner's attitude; 2) terminate the relationship; 3) find a middle ground. How do you think this couple compromised?

Anna and Winston entered into a second marriage while in their late sixties, after their spouses had died. Both came from a traditional, conservative background and tried to impress that upon each other during their courtship.

Winston assumed that Anna would want the more dependent, look-to-the-man role; all money matters would be in his hands. Having been a widower for a few years and the breadwinner all his life, he inwardly yearned to be taken care of a little himself. Anna had truly been protected in her first marriage of forty years. Her first husband paid the bills, and invested without consulting Anna on the details. She respected that he was a good provider and she made the family income stretch. Secretly, she resented the role she played and daydreamed about a career as an assertive business woman, raking in the cash. Winston and Anna swallowed their deepest desires and married for companionship. As they dealt with their finances in their familiar routine, resentment built up. They then sought counseling and began to communicate the truth about money to each other. The last I heard, Anna had a profitable little boutique business and Winston appreciated the extra "good life" it provided them.

The Power of Money

Money has incredible power over people. When is enough, enough? I have friends who charge items much like an alcoholic drinks, to assuage pain. Money's addictive quality throws a couple's lives into chaos. Be sure to address your values regarding *debts*. There are times when disagreements over spending or saving can strain an otherwise good relationship. When you don't have enough money and choices need to be made, the differences in values intensify. You may feel that building an addition to a new house is more important than the cruise the two of you were hoping to take. On the other hand, your partner may want to indulge and live dangerously for a week and believes the time is now or never.

Situations like this cause tremendous stress in a relationship. Who is right? Who wins? It had better be a *win-win* situation or you both lose. Compromise is the name of the game.

Goals and Financial Planning

A goal is an end toward which effort is directed—to go back to college, to put away a nest-egg for the kids' education, to renovate the house. Goals change as we change, so couples need to continually reevaluate. Goals always give a purpose in living and motivation to keep a steady course.

Personal Goals and Money

Usually, you don't have the money to make your dreams come true. Maybe partially. And maybe not right away. Look at where you are today and the things you have, then ask yourself what you want. The first step toward a goal is *identifying* it. Then *define* it and be *specific.*

Maybe your *goal* is to becme a well-off entrepreneur. Too general! "I will own my own catering service business where I will generate maybe ten thousand a year," is more apt self-talk to get you to your goal.

Mutual Goals

When the two of you become one in the sacrament of marriage, something has to give. It's fine to have and support a personal goal, especially if you are a two paycheck family. In a single wage-earner family, you must consider your partner's input.

Your goals should have three components:

1. Direction—Where do we want to go?
2. Resources—How can we get there?
3. Time—When do we expect to get there?

In our society we have low frustration tolerance. As I stated at the beginning of this chapter, young couples splurge for the reception and honeymoon, often pulling on the money aprons of their parents (who could never have afforded such splendor in their day). Big doesn't always mean better, and simplicity can be beautiful.

Budgeting the Basics

A budget is a plan for spending money and an essential tool that helps you reach your goals. Be sure your goals take into account your wants and your needs. Our society sinfully defines us by what we own, not by who we are. If you wear this perfume, or drive that make of car, if you drink this brand of beer, or eat that diet slush you will be happy, according to the world. As a couple sorts their basic needs from their trivial and selfish wants, they can plan a more realistic budget.

Making a Budget

When you were a lone ranger, budgeting was relatively easy. Now, with communication and compromise, you review your priorities. Some considerations that partners need to discuss include:

Are you both working full time?
Will this continue even if you start a family?

The first step in creating a budget is listing all available income. How much are you paid each month? Then there are three types of expenses you will need to track: fixed, flexible and periodic.

Fixed expenses deal with the costs of living that come each month, such as rent, credit card payments and savings. Record keeping is easy here.

Flexible expenses are necessities, too, but you can

play with them a bit. Food, clothing, transportation and entertainment come under this umbrella.

Periodic expenses can be both fixed and flexible. Taxes, car insurance and car maintenance fall into this category.

Experts say that savings are an important part of budgeting! That rainy day may come, or an emergency may strike, and you may be glad you put away some portion of your income every month.

Decide who will be responsible for paying bills and keeping records. Delegate or share the chore, but be clear about who has what responsibility.

Sermon on the Mount

Stewardship is a key word for Christians. It means that *all* is gift: time, talent and money to put at God's disposal. Since God will require an accounting (Mt 25, 31-46) at the end of our lives, the Lord is where the buck will stop. Do you as a couple feed the hungry and clothe the naked with the resources you have available? Do you remember the radical challenge of the Lord to all disciples: "It is easier for a camel to go through the eye of a needle than for a rich person to enter the kingdom of God." Do we realize that even if we are poor in wages here, we are richer than most people on the planet?

Dennis and Michelle live by the biblical principle of tithing. They allocate the *top ten* percent of their income to the Lord's work: a certain percent to their parish, the needs of the poor in their diocese, local charities and personal causes that promote peace and justice.

"The T.V. evangelists who sell the 'gospel of health and wealth' equate prosperity with God's blessing," complains Michelle. "They ignore the message of the cross and the call of Jesus to see him in the least," she protests.

Dennis rightly insists that the sacrament of marriage bestows "couple power," and part of that energy must be available to the needy.

So, in values, in goal setting and budgeting all Christian couples must hear the cry of the poor in whatever form they present themselves in today's society. At the last judgment I have a theory that God will call each married couple to a great *audit*. "Whatever you did to the least, you did to me."

DISCUSSION QUESTIONS

1. What would you call living a "good life?"
   How much money do you think that will require?

2. What are our immediate financial goals?

3. What are our long-range financial goals?

6

Can Love Grow?

I guess you could say I'm a love-researcher, looking for love in all the right places. As a parish priest, I witness the evolution of our species, and love is the catalyst. From the womb to the tomb, people teach me the art of loving. Sometimes the art is a bit primitive, sometimes a masterpiece, always worth the price. Let me illustrate.

I walk into a first-grade classroom and quiz my resident philosophers with the rhetorical question: "What is love?" they don't hesitate to share their wisdom. They extend their arm as far as they can stretch, as if to say, "Mommy loves me *this* much." Somehow, their all-embracing gesture says everything.

Another time, on a cold winter day, I found three little neighbor kids on the church steps, all about the age of four. The little girl had a runny nose, which didn't seem to concern her two male companions. Since they were about to enter the building for their religion lesson, I said, teasingly, "What would Jesus want you to do for your friend with the runny nose?" Again, without uttering a word, one little boy matter-of-factly offered the sleeve of his coat. What a sermon!

So, these little children teach us that love is wide-open and trusting, it means offering whatever works—maybe your sleeve.

At another time, I approached the fifth graders with

my question, "What is love?" They squirm, giggle and make weird noises with their armpits. I get the message.

I later quiz the eighth graders, "What is love?: This time one boy in the back pulls out a suggestive picture from the *Sports Illustrated* swimsuit issue, and bellows, "*this* is love." The eighth grade girls remark condescendingly, "Whatever love is, it's *not* one of them," pointing to the pint-sized boys.

Curiously, in the junior year, my question meets a dead silence, and the kids hang their head down or look at me as if to ask, "What do you know?" My hunch: by this stage all of them are either "in love," been looking for love, or been burnt by love.

I wish you could sit with me during the first interview of a couple who have come to get acquainted with me and set a wedding date.

It might go like this:

"Is he working?"

"No, but my love for him will get him going."

"Does she have any bad habit you are concerned about?"

"Yes, she drinks too much, hasn't grown up yet, and doesn't believe in God...but my love will change her."

A bit naive, huh? Well, time will pop their bubble. A friend of mine, who wanted to sail on the Love Boat for her honeymoon is now a settled-in wife and mother of two boys. She laments her figure while her two urchins cling to her dress, and warns, "This is what love does!"

When the empty nest syndrome hits, a man and woman face each other squarely and wonder, "Now that the kids are gone, can we recapture that love we knew in those early days?"

Love in the twilight years? Yes, I've seen it. There are

some couples I know, married fifty or more years, still holding hands at social events.

The Websters led healthy, robust married lives until three years ago when Mr. Webster showed signs of Alzheimer's. Now he is visited each Sunday by his wife who dresses him in his finest suit and escorts him on their traditional Sunday stroll. I look at them, how they keep their dignity, how precious their time together is, even without words, and I know how deep love can go.

Read the Fine Print

A lawyer friend of mine cautions me to read the fine print in any contract or document so I won't get hoodwinked. My doctor always warns me to read the fine print on the medicine bottle label so I won't mix the wrong medicines. Yet, it seems the only one who tells us to read the fine print when it come to love is God.

The Lord admonishes, "Love can be hazardous to your health. Never tell someone you love them unless you mean it, and never mean it unless you mean it forever." (my paraphrase)

We will take a closer look at the meaning of the vows in the next chapter.

Schedule Quality Time

Married couples tell me that it helps to like the one you love. Quality time together helps the cause. Brandon changed his hectic life with a course on time-management. He seemed to be running in circles, spewing a lot of steam but accomplishing nothing. When he got his work straightened out by learning to prioritize, he thought, "Why not make quality time for the most important investment of my life?" His wife, Eileen, had grown accustomed to his leftover time: a quick lunch at a fast food place, a fast cup of coffee and a peck on the cheek in the morning, maybe a little exchange at night, after an exhausting day—could there be more? She had settled into a comfortable life-style, but there was little intimacy, fun or romance in their marriage—the qualities that make love grow.

Brandon, coming to his senses at last, called an executive meeting with his wife. He said, "Read my lips, we're going to make the quality of our marriage *top priority*!" After Eileen got over the shock, they brainstormed ways to maximize their time together. They would get up an hour earlier and talk about the day ahead, not just the facts and itinerary, but the way they *felt* about the events of the day. Talking "heart to heart" gave them a positive attitude toward each other, and the good vibes even flowed over to the people in the work place, making lots of people a little less stressed.

This new arrangement worked so well that they devoted one hour in the evening to go for an uninterrupted walk together. Instead of doing their couch potato ritual in front of the T.V., they got reacquainted after twenty years. Scheduling quality time together makes love grow.

Be Creative

Couples tell me that a little mystery in a marriage spices things up. Nobody wants to be taken for granted and everybody loves surprises. Look what Wendy and Clark Peterson cooked up. According to Wendy....

"We take turns coming up with an original treat for one another. *Monday* is our 'surprise day'. One week I might cook up his favorite dinner, the next week it's his turn to please me. Recently, he took me dancing. While some people dread Mondays, it's the highlight of our week. We have agreed to schedule that night as our date. We get baby-sitters and allow no interruptions. Building expectancy into our marriage has added spice."

Plan Celebrations

We consecrate special times, places and events to celebrate how much a person means to us. It is very important for married couples to incorporate parties, big and small, into their yearly, monthly, weekly and daily routine. Aside from birthdays and anniversaries, how about making the ordinary extraordinary!

Celebrations to mark: Your first promotion.
Your first house.
Your first news of parenthood.
Your first fight (and make-up).
Your first paycheck.
Your first box of parish
envelopes.

So often we focus on the negatives in life and get little joy out of the real successes in front of our noses. Congratulate yourselves for the times you resolved a conflict amicably, and reward yourselves suitably for surviving intact particularly stressful times together.

Your celebrations can be marked by a pizza on a Friday night, a weekend away, or the simple exchange of homemade cards (as one couple I know relishes). You don't have to spend money, but you do need to tell each other what you're doing right, and do it often. Celebrations pull you out of the rut and help love grow.

Be Daring

A recent commercial on T.V. illustrates the sameness of some marriages. An elderly couple go into a fast-food place to order lunch. The old gentlemen shuffles to the counter and ever-so-slowly requests his usual hamburger and fries. His wife flashes an angry look his way, and in an exasperated tone says, "Live a little, take a chance; you order the same thing every day; get in the ball game, for God's sake."

Get in the ball game, couples.

I've known marriages that have died of boredom. And yet, I know others who tackle a team project or hobby *together*. Blanche and Rod were such a couple. Devoted parents of teenagers, they refused to invest all their energy in them. They took a course in public speaking at the nearby college and had loads of fun coaching each other.

Again, another couple in my parish accepted the challenge of tutoring an elderly couple in a literacy program, and gained more than they invested. The focus outside themselves prevented obsessing about the petty stuff at home.

Whether you try high adventure or simply try on a new hobby, couples interested in life make better lovers.

A Little Help from Your Friends

In a coffee shop near where I live, one sees the adage "birds of a feather flock together." You have a lobbying group at every table. At one table, in the corner, a group of unhappy divorcees commiserate. Anyone within earshot catches their drift: they *hate* marriage. Each one bitterly complains about the price they paid to gain their freedom. Each tries to tell a better horror story about marital infidelity than the other. The moral: *marry and burn.*

I knew a young couple who developed bad habits early. After six months, Clyde decided to hang out "just a little" with his bachelor buddies again. "Little" became regular, and regular led to irregular hours, and then trouble at the ranch. Monica decided to play the same game. So, she had her "girls night out," living a single life while wearing a wedding ring—just like her husband. The marriage ended in divorce.

By all means, pick friends who believe in marriage, who are not out to pull you down to their level of misery. Don't kid yourself about socializing mainly with folks in the single life-style. Their values and priorities differ markedly from yours. Couples will usually gravitate to couples their own age, but I have seen special friendships develop for young couples with a more mature pair who serve as role models or mentors. Hopefully, your parish will provide a healthy network of married friends. If not, *you* get something going. Married love grows where married love is nurtured.

Love and the Paschal Mystery

"Dying your destroyed our death, Rising your restored our life, Lord Jesus, come in glory." We acclaim words like these at every eucharist. It is the paschal mystery: out of death comes life. This is also the meaning of love for Catholic Christians who believe in the sacrament of marriage. Let's figure out what it means in everyday marital reality.

To be weak and vulnerable before another, comes with intimacy. We naturally set up defenses, because who wants to be hurt? In marriage a person must die to that kind of protectiveness so love can grow.

Like so many, Nan came from a dysfunctional family. She had been verbally abused throughout her childhood, so learning to trust her husband, Tim, she had to risk assertiveness without fear of retaliation. Her faith told her that her husband could be an instrument of the Lord's healing. In her willingness to be vulnerable to Tim, she died; in her dying, a life was born for both of them.

Dave always struggled with his ego. By his own admission, he was a poor sport. He never gave an inch and often took a mile. Before his marriage to Rose, he had a deep conversion experience. he learned how to say the magic words, "I'm sorry," "Forgive me." He died to self and, learning how to compromise, rose to new heights in married love.

When asked whether love can grow, the Christian answers a resounding *yes*. This happens by reading the fine print about quality time, creativity, celebrations, courage, good friends and the paschal mystery.

DISCUSSION QUESTIONS

1. What roadblocks have we already met that prevent us from making time for each others?

2. How can we overcome these roadblocks?

7

Sticking It Out

Recently, I took a group of engaged couples on a flight of fantasy. We used no mantra, no hypnosis, just a chalkboard, a blank piece of paper and pencil. On the board, I printed in bold letters: I GIVE MYSELF TO YOU IN GOOD DAYS, IN BAD DAYS, FOR RICHER OR POORER, IN SICKNESS AND IN HEALTH—ALL THE DAYS OF MY LIFE. Then we let our imaginations go wild and put on paper whatever came to mind after each key phrase. You will be interested in reviewing the outpouring of thoughts and feelings about their vows.

I Give Myself to You

"But will you like me when you see me close up?"
"How can I give what I don't have?"
"You asked for it!"
"That's the most unselfish thing I've ever said!"
"And don't you hurt me."
"Maybe not all of me, but most of me."

Actually, the exact wording of that first phrase is "I *take* you..."—too aggressive for me. Marriage is not about conquest, but *surrender*. I share this list with happily married couples who validated the concerns echoed.

Always, in dating and in engagement, persons hold back a little of themselves. Only slowly and cautiously, always testing the waters, does the real person come out. And true enough, as suggested in earlier chapters, a person with little sense of personal identity and self-worth will weigh down the partner with impossible demands. That handsome hunk of man sleeping next to you could lose his hair, and gain a pot belly. That raving beauty snuggled in your arms might snore, or expel gas at the most inopportune times. You will find out that you did not get quite what you asked for; that nicely wrapped package holds damaged goods.

I don't need to burst your bubble. Time will do that. It's only a matter of time before bad breath, poor manners, little eccentricities and fading good looks will destroy your illusions. But then, you're no prize, either. So, relax. The real adventure begins when you stop posing for each other, and intimacy has a way of speeding up the process. But you can't run for the hills at the sign of the first blemish. Stay for the rush of real discovery.

I asked my grandmother once how long it took her to "fall in love" with grandpa. She protested that she never fell into anything in her life. She *decided* to give herself to him unconditionally, and fully expected he would return the compliment.

In Good Days

"When we have our own house."
"When I cook better than your mom."
"When the children come."
"When the children go."
"When we make dreams come true."
"When I'm there to support you."

So goes the list on the *good days*. Would you believe that good things can be stressful! Folks who've won a fortune in the lottery have been known to join support groups to deal with the headaches of being rich and famous. (You'd gladly catch that virus, right?)

Sometimes, the motto of newlyweds sounds like the theme of the early civil rights movements: "Thank God, I'm *free* at last, *free* at last!" You sure are, and that's got to make you feel good all over. You can now make your own mistakes and take the consequences. And there is something exhilarating about being in charge of your destiny—well, almost.

In the small town where I pastor, I see couples very excited about building their own house. I'm not handy at all, so I marvel at the skill these young couples have in all facets of construction and decorating. Sitting in my rectory parlor, they sparkle as they describe their dream house. I do worry, though, when they believe all good things must come at once. That's when credit card mania can rear its ugly head. Anyway, you have to see the joy on the faces of couples who are doing their own thing their own way.

Yes, in the beginning, *comparisons* are made. Maybe mom made an unbelievable bowl of chili. And no matter how hard you try, you just can't duplicate the flavor. Why not have a good time experimenting? You might accidentally discover a concoction that your in-laws would envy. And, if you can't make anything but burnt toast now, have lots of laughs and know that necessity is the mother of invention.

What a thrill for me to visit with a new father, right after he coached his wife in labor and witnessed the miracle of birth. To celebrate first communions, first confessions, first anything with families is the thrill of priesthood. Those are the finest days.

Down the road I also see couples bid a fond farewell to their kids. It's not that raising, chauffeuring, refereeing, and counseling kids isn't good; it's just that it's *very good* to be alone with each other. True, the empty nest has it's challenges, but it does present some golden opportunities to renew your love for each other.

Couples often remember fondly their dreams of yesterday as the "good ole days." I know a well-to-do middle-aged couple who didn't always have it so good. And you know what? They miss those tougher times when luxuries were scarce and common dreams united them. When pressed, they admit they miss those long talks late into the night when they dreamt about owning an elegant restaurant. In those days, they did without individually so they could reach their common goal. And every step, however small, toward that goal flooded their days with excitement. How sad that, when dreams come true, people sometimes turn off the creative juices and don't dream anymore.

Couples who love each other know that on those really good days of marriage, knowing and feeling the *support* of the other made all the difference. It could come as one spouse decides to go back to school, and the other gladly shoulders most of the financial and family burden for awhile. It could come as a mate takes an assertive stand at work and the other cheers him or her on. It might mean you want to take the plunge of joining the Order of Christian Initiation of Adults in your parish, and your spouse, the Catholic party, wants to attend all the sessions with you. It might mean a clear refusal to have your kids play one of you against the other, or milk you dry with all their attention-grabbing. Whatever the case, however it gets translated, your children will know you are *one*.

Yes, you vow those good days to each other: looking at sunsets, celebrating promotions, enjoying a good movie, sharing ideas, laughing with each other at your foolishness, and so much more. And those good days help you to stick it out.

In Bad Days

How bad is bad? And how much of a bad thing can one take? Bad could mean when good goes sour. Again, listen in on these comments:

"If you lose your job..."
"If we have a really bad fight..."
"If we don't like each other..."
"If we stop communication..."

A Greek philosopher once said that it is not reality but how we interpret it that makes or breaks us. Why do some couples I meet see the glass half-full while others swear it's half-empty?

For the Christian, bad breaks are not lightning bolts sent to punish a naughty child, nor are disciples of Jesus magically spared setbacks. Bad days come in different packages, all signed with a card that reads *loss*.

How a couple rebounds from loss—even more important, how they perceive it as the end or the beginning—will be grace or tragedy.

The Ryans lived a low-middle-class life-style, with the husband the sole wage-earner. When he lost his job, the two felt panic; after panic, helplessness; after helplessness, depression. They took out their frustration and worry on each other and became, for a time, verbally abusive. They sought pastoral counseling and turned their misdirected anger to more constructive channels. He found a number of part-time jobs and she went to work outside the home. Slowly, Bud Ryan's attitude to this misfortune as "all bad," turned to focusing on the positive of bonding with his children while he had to play house dad. The family made new rules about recreational spending, and resolved to be friends, not sparring partners through this ordeal. To see only the dark side of a situation and not the *challenge* will doom a couple to awful days together until the storm passes.

Yes, sometimes you will say things you regret in the heat of battle. So, stop short of saying those things you can never take back, and make your argument a learning experience. How can you turn a lose-lose into a win-win situation? By learning how to brainstorm options and by mastering conflict resolution skills (have the parish offer workshops!), your tiffs can deepen intimacy—once you *fight fair*.

Don't expect to always like each other. Take some time to get perspective, cool off, talk to a friend before you head for a lawyer. It's not horrendous to have negative feelings for your partner. Explore those feelings together, use this impasse as a teacher, not an enemy. Conflict and occasional intense feelings of dislike are an inevitable part of joining two separate individuals together. It doesn't automatically assume the end is near.

In Sickness and in Health

To watch someone you love suffer, and feel helpless, goes with the territory. It's part of reading the fine print in the marriage vows. Sooner or later one of you will have to be on the receiving end of love, while the other does most of the giving.

When Patty lost her breasts to cancer, she feared rejection from Mark. After all, he had always teased that her body still turned him on after forty years of marriage. Would she now be desirable or disgusting, she wondered.

Mark showed special tenderness to his wife after the operation and during recovery. He held her in his arms and reassured her that he found her sensuous because of how she was, and how it hurt him to have her doubt it.

Truthfully, I do know relationships that have broken up because of the strain of dealing with deformities or strokes. We all read about a spouse putting a gun to the head of an invalid mate to kill the pain for both of them.

Please discuss with your spouse your wishes if you are left in a state where extraordinary means are needed to keep you alive. Don't be in denial. Talk to each other *now*.

Our parishes often provide vibrant programs for healthy young couples. I don't believe we offer much at all for stressed-out family members during serious or prolonged illness. I know we offer nothing in terms of support for a man or woman living with a mentally ill loved one.

I don't believe that pastoral leaders should claim expertise where they have none. But I do believe the research shows great promise for *support groups* of all kinds. We should have them in all our parishes for couples who cope with debilitating illness. The church witnessed the vows of that hurting couple when they promised fidelity in sickness and health. We cannot stand idly by and only remember them at the prayers of the faithful at mass.

All the Days of My Life

I often ask at a funeral whether loving that person for umpteen years was worth the pain of final separation. The answer always comes back *yes*. Of course, my faith tells me that the final word is life, not death, for the faithful disciple. Resurrection IS the GRAND FINALE.

DISCUSSION QUESTIONS

1. In your opinion, why do some marriages fail?

2. What makes a successful marriage?
   What is your role in a successful marriage?
   What is the role of your partner in a successful marriage?

8

Dirty Thoughts

Now that I've got your attention, I would like you to focus your mind on thoughts that all of us think which are particularly detrimental to marriage. As we *think*, so we *feel*, so we *do*. It's true that change in one area affects change in another. I will single out what I call "dirty thoughts" as culprits.

Thought No. 1: "You've Got E.S.P."

Maybe you are psychic; then skip this part. If you're like most of us, you can't read minds. Unless you are clear and specific about your wants and needs, you will not get them met, and you might blame your partner for insensitivity.

Ruth and Jack appeared in my office one day wearing two different facial expressions. Ruth had a wide-eyed, outraged look; Jack had a blank stare of disbelief.

"What brings you here?"

"Jack knows I want a divorce and he knows why," scowled Ruth.

"But, honey, I have no idea why you want a divorce; tell me," he begged.

"If you loved me, you'd know," she retorted.

"We've both established that I am a good provider, a

good lover, a good father, and your best friend—so why in God's name do you want to divorce me?"

This is the actual transcript of the initial exchange, and it never got any more focused. Mind reading doesn't cut it, yet, to my amazement, couples build resentments and hold grudges with this kind of fuzzy thinking. Just ask questions like:

"What did you mean by that word?"
"Why did you say that in such a tone?"
"You look like you're telling me something with your body language. .. am I reading you right?"
"Let's just talk *now* about what happened, so I don't read into your actions, okay?"

Such a reality-based line of questioning will save needless brooding that comes with false assumptions.

Thought No. 2: "You're All Bad/All Good"

As I've intimated throughout this book, nobody is or gets a perfect model of humanity. No one is all villain or saint. To tag someone as the epitome of either is to set up an impossible living situation. "Jeremy doesn't have the faith," his wife bemoans. "But he attends mass with you every week, participates in parish life, and visits shut-ins," I counter-argue with his wife, Emily.

As it turns out, Emily has had a profound religious experience at a prayer group in recent months, and now can't get enough of the Bible. She has become almost fanatical in her insistence that he devour the scriptures the way she does. In her badgering of this man, she is alienating him and overlooking his fine qualities. The marriage could rupture at any time.

Larry, to use another example, despises his wife Vanessa's annoying habit of nail-biting. A nervous woman, she has bitten her nails until her fingers bleed and certainly could use some professional help to change this habit. But she is not a bad person because she does this, as Larry implies, and she has many redeeming features which he overlooks: an excellent cook, good listener, excellent homemaker, good joke teller. Instead of celebrating and affirming those qualities of the woman he married, he paints her as a complete neurotic, and, of course, has induced some nail-biting sessions in the process.

Such perfectionistic thinking causes depression and anxiety and produces self-defeating behavior. Sometimes *good* is good enough.

Thought No. 3: "Making It Personal"

Freud, who analyzed everything, was confronted by a peer about the inner meaning of his smoking habit. His response: "Sometimes a cigar is just a cigar."

Your lifelong companion does "stew" over more things than just you. If he was late for dinner, it doesn't necessarily mean he rejects you. Maybe the boss accosted him, the traffic piled up, he was a good Samaritan to a grandmother with a flat tire. Ask him!

When she doesn't warm up to your romantic advances, it may not mean she finds the thirty extra pounds you've gained repulsive. The incessant demand for attention from the kids that day may have pushed her to the breaking point and she just wants to be left alone. Could that be an alternative explanation for her behavior?

Illness, worry, frustration, biochemical imbalance, a shouting match with a Jehovah Witness, all this and more can shape a person's response.

So, check it out, ask questions, back off a while, don't presume it's aimed at you. Sometimes a cigar is just a cigar and a cold look comes from a cold draft.

Thought No. 4: Giving Labels

"A rose by any other name is still a rose." Is it? Somehow, I don't think it would smell the same if I called it an onion. Take some of these classic labels I've heard tossed about by couples:

"She is a dingbat."
"He is a child."
"She is a loser."
"He is a slob."
"She is a clown."
"He is a nerd."

I have known three dogs in my life who have given me a lesson in human psychology. The first, "Fang," chased me, mercilessly, up a tree and kept me imprisoned there for an hour. When the owner returned, he dismissed the bloodthirsty hound and cautioned me that the last priest who visited still had nightmares.

Then there was "Meathead," a mutt the fraternity boys owned at the graduate school I attended. This dog sat when you said "down" and ran the other way when you said "come." He was as harmless as he was stupid.

The third, I have at my side as I write this—"Buddy." He jumps with joy at the first glance of a stranger (a possible playmate), brings you a toy and my socks as a token of friendship when you enter my house, and lies at your feet all during your visit with me.

In all three cases, I've suspected the *label* given to each pet shaped its personality. This is no scientific hypothesis but a workable hunch. A label affects the way we treat anything. Call something or someone mean, stupid or friend often enough and you might get whom you called for.

Couples need to not equate an action, incident or trait with the whole person. She might act "dingily" at times but she's not a dingbat. He might be childish at times, but he's not a child. She might lose every now and then, but that doesn't make her a loser. He may occasionally—okay, more than occasionally—act sloppily, but that doesn't mean he's a certified slob. She may clown around, but she can be serious, too. He may behave "nerdily" but a nerd he is not. When we give our loved ones labels, we think dirty thoughts. And when we think dirty thoughts we get in trouble.

Thought No. 5: "Should've, Would've, Could've, Some Day Syndrome"

If you owned a time machine, where would you travel? If you had your choice, would you take a ride down memory lane, to a time when your marriage was better? Or, would you fly off to the future somewhere over the rainbow?

Max and Mindy would entertain me with their scrapbooks at every pastoral visit. It seemed those first five years were the best, all thirty years after paled by comparison. Life was simpler then, kids were cute, health was a given. They then end our conversation with their "should've" list:

"We *should've* saved more; look at us know."

"We *should've* been tougher with the kids; look at the mess their lives are in."

"We *should've* taken that job in the city."

"We *should've* never made that investment."

Now, the Talbots, another couple I visit, give themselves an "A" for potential, while I would score them an "F" for effort.

Their woe list goes like this;

"We *would've* made our marriage work, had we had our relatives at our side."

"We *would've* taken vacations together but we didn't have the time."

"We *would've* not changed so much if we knew then what we know now."

The Waltons, a couple married ten years, mirror the could've syndrome. Listen:

"We *could've* both gotten degrees had we started earlier."

"We *could've* enjoyed the kids more when they were younger."

"We *could've* traveled more when we were healthier, but didn't."

"We *could've* practiced our faith better as young adults, then maybe we wouldn't feel so lost today."

In all these scenarios we hear regrets about yesterday. As long as couples think these dirty thoughts, today might slip through their hands, too.

A variation on the same theme of regret, but with a futuristic twist, is the word someday.

"Now we can't communicate but *someday* we will."

"Now we can't get involved in church but *someday* we will."

"Now we can't take time for ourselves but *someday* we will."

By putting off quality time, better communication, and faith commitment until tomorrow, couples rob today of its power. "Someday" is no better than playing yesterday's frustrated dreams over in the tape deck of our minds.

Dirty thinking produces feelings of despair and futility which, in turn, produces inaction.

So, whether you think dirty, mind read, personalize, are a perfectionist or label, change your internal scripts so your marriage has a chance. Your partner will thank you.

DISCUSSION QUESTIONS

1. What characteristics about your partner do you most admire? Why? Do you possess these same characteristics? How are we similar? How are we different?

2. What negative "tapes" do I play for myself?

3. How can I help my partner to be the best that he or she can be?

4. What must I do for myself to achieve my full potential?

9

Spirituality

Corita and Arnie stunned me: Could they possibly do what they say they do on a date? Pray together. "In high school we went on a retreat together and learned how to pray spontaneously. Feeling a little awkward at first, we tried praying the "Our Father" together before we'd start up the car. Not long into our relationship we put prayer into our own words, and spoke to the Lord out loud *together*. We prayed about anything and everything: our families, our friends, the world scene, help in temptation—let me tell you, prayer changed the tone of our date." So they reported to me.

Countless couples testify that *prayer together* strengthens their bond. Some begin their day with a morning offering, consecrating all the joys and sufferings of the day to God. Others end their day with prayers of petition and thanksgiving. Older, retired couples I know start off their day with morning mass, followed by a leisurely breakfast. A luxury they couldn't indulge in with a schedule of work and kids, now sanctifies their remaining years.

Neil and Constance decided to enroll in a *bible study* group in their parish. For years they bowled and golfed together and, as much fun as that was, nothing compared to the joy of discovering how God's word cast a new light on the ordinary events of life.

Clark and Delores involved themselves in a weekly *charismatic prayer group*, which enhanced their liturgical life in the parish and gave them a new appreciation for the gifts of the Spirit.

Helen and Trent, deeply indebted to the *Marriage Encounter Movement* for renewing their relationship, emerged as leaders in recruiting other couples.

Spirituality is about a deeper walk with the Lord—including Christ as a partner in the marriage. The media distorts intimacy by reducing it to raw sex. Real intimacy, as these couples attest, involves the dynamic interconnection of the psychological, physical, emotional *and* spiritual dimensions of two people.

Covenant

Legal contracts can intimidate and protect the self-interests of one party, but nothing rings sacred about them. Covenant, a biblical term, bases the relationship on God's terms—which spell fidelity over the long haul. Both the Lord and the parties covenanted make promises. God promises to protect and grace the bond: the couples promise to live their love guided by God's commandments and beatitudes.

Sin occurs when the covenant is breached and that is always unilateral—our doing.

I need to interject here that I have counseled many couples pastorally and a number in clinical settings: Sin *does* have something to do with divorce!

I recall a married man who came to see me in my role as therapist in a family mental health agency. He did not know I was a priest and I did not play that role. He listed physical complaints: pounding headaches, ulcers, diarrhea, rashes, irritability, restlessness. A medical exam ruled out anything organic as a cause for his discomfort, and so the doctor recommended individual counseling.

I tried everything over a period of six months: behavior modification, cognitive therapy, delving into his past childhood, active listening, family and marital therapy sessions. Nothing helped. One day, toward the end of a session, out of desperation, I asked, "Is there *anything* you feel guilty about?" He held his head down and cried, "I have a mistress." What this man needed was a chance to get to the sacrament of reconciliation (he was Catholic); not until his real guilt was addressed would he recover.

Of course, pastoral leaders and parish people must use the utmost sensitivity in treating divorced people. Sometimes so much damage has happened that divorce is the only solution. Then the church must make room, help in the grieving process and facilitate healing. But I have also seen too many good people dumped by a partner, causing tremendous pain for the whole family. I will not be part of the conspiracy of silence in never calling divorce—breaking of the covenant—sin. Just as I will never stop being a companion for those who must pick up their lives and go on.

Marriage as Sacrament

I love being a Catholic because the sacraments bring that human touch. If there is anything Catholics do well it's *consecrate*. We say the Lord's words over water, oil, bread, wine, buildings, and people. The meaning we attach to anything or anybody we consecrate changes that reality forever. In a sacrament the risen Lord meets us, faith is presupposed, conversion happens, the parish community embraces us, and the world is offered hope.

I have a confession to make and I may get in hot water

if I tell it. Then again, it might catch on. Before the final blessing, during the nuptial mass, I kneel before the couple, who are now a *sacrament*, and ask for *their* blessing (in silence). I find this sacramental gesture stirs the couple and congregation beyond words.

When two Catholic Christians marry, they administer the sacrament to each other. The rest of the church, including the priest witness that consecration.

Grace

Each sacrament confers its special grace for the living out of that calling. I'm not sure most couples realize what that means for their daily lives together. (I have recently come to appreciate the guaranteed helps that goes with my sacrament of holy orders, reminded by married people, I might add.)

Let me illustrate how Marshall and his wife Sharon have experienced grace in the nitty-gritty. According to Sharon, "When Marshall sat me down to break the news that his invalid mother was going to live with us, I cried. She had never liked me, had always kept her distance, and somehow poisoned the rest of his family against me. Now her serious illness and the death of her husband left her dependent. My husband was in a better financial condition than his brothers, so he volunteered our home for six months of the year. I consented but knew the burden of her care would fall on me. I worried that our marriage might crack under the stress."

So did they cope?

"We are Catholics who claim the promises God made on our wedding day. We believe that God is *solution-oriented;* that's what 'grace' means. So we prayed and looked for strength and the resources to grow stronger through this," says Sharon.

"Grace is nothing magical," insists Marshall, "but it means *expectant faith*. We trusted that if circumstances wouldn't turn around, *we* would! And we did. My wife reached out to my mother in a new way. My mother was touched by her concern, fully aware of how she had treated Sharon over the years. They became friends. I shared the responsibility and grew to love my wife more because of those two years we gave to mom." Grace at work!

Bruce and Lily prized parenting as their greatest task. They made quality time for each of their four daughters, listened attentively to them, drew boundaries, and modeled an active life of faith. They talked freely about sex and sexuality with their daughters, and talked to them together. They held traditional values which conflicted with society's permissiveness. Yet, they were not prudes; all their kids saw healthy affection and joy in their parents' marriage.

When their youngest daughter announced she was pregnant, the world caved in. Her plans for college, her dreams for a career in music, all came to a screeching halt.

Listen to the stand Bruce and Lily took toward their daughter, with God's grace. "We know that we are not bad parents. We have a lot of competition out there and, bottom line, our daughter is a free agent. We relied upon God's grace, offered on our wedding day, to turn this darkness into light. We were so glad our daughter ruled out abortion, and was willing to make an informed decision about adoption. We said we loved her the way Christ loved all of us—unconditionally. And some remarkable people began to appear in our life to support and encourage and guide all of us. In our decision-making process we were not alone. God's grace sent the right people, with the right words, at the right time."

So, what is this grace God bestowed on you when you entered a covenant and became a sacrament?

Know this: in your married life a mystery will be at work, reminding you of your vows, breaking down your defenses, drawing you away from your selfishness, bringing supportive people into your life, and stripping you of illusions. This is God's grace at work.

Vocation to Holiness

No one has a monopoly on holiness. The myth of priests and religious having a corner on sanctity is debunked with each scandal that makes the papers. I am in awe as I see the face of Christ in the joys, sufferings and glories of the married vocation. In fact, married people have taught me how needed is the witness of celibate love to highlight the vertical dimension to God's love, as they mirror the horizontal.

Married people must communicate more than just feelings to each other. They need to talk about their individual walks with the Lord. Questions like, "How is your personal prayer life?" and "What is God saying to you in the personal events of your day?" should grace a couple's conversation. It would be important to encourage each other to celebrate the sacrament of reconciliation frequently, and to facilitate private prayer time and retreats for the other. One day each spouse will answer to God for the opportunities or roadblocks he or she places in the path of their partner's journey to God.

Couple Power

There is strength in numbers, and in the case of married vocation, the power number is *two*. As indicated in a previous chapter, your marriage isn't just for you. In a world that talks of tying the knot and biting the bullet, Jesus calls you "light of the world" and "salt of the earth."

The poor need you. Perhaps children are waiting for *you* to adopt them. Engaged couples need role models to mentor them. Our society needs happily married people to advocate for family values, the simple life, quality of life and justice for the vulnerable. We need couples to be evangelists, calling back Catholic couples who have drifted away or withered away from the church. You have power to initiate, confirm, heal, reconcile and confront. Use this power of your sacrament to bring light into the darkness and seasoning to the world gone flat.

DISCUSSION QUESTIONS

1. How important is faith *now* in our relationship?

2. Is our relationship drawing us closer to God or farther away? Why?

10

Mixed Marriages

What I see of religious "formation" in the couples who come for marital instruction is quite a mix, indeed. They come culturally Catholic, loosely Catholic, confused Catholic, grudgingly Catholic, "New-age" Catholic, yet all claiming Catholic as their family name. Their prospective spouse has no religion, a deeply committed fundamentalist religion, an anti-Catholic religion, a-little-bit-of-everything religion. Usually, faith is not the highest priority on their agenda of discussion items (it ranks at the bottom of the list—just before, "How much does the church cost?")

I have a question for the couples who see me: "Do they realize how important a part faith, church affiliation and religious differences will play later in their marriage?"

Turning Catholic

Someone's grandfather must have warned Rex not to sign anything in my office he would regret later. Dianna, his fiancée, spoke for him.

"Rex wants to turn Catholic someday, so don't worry."

"But, Dianna, it's *you*, I'm worried about. Your parents are registered here, but I *never* see you at mass. I'd like you to 'turn Catholic' first."

"You're right, Father, But the last priest was *sooo* boring, and the priest before that yelled at babies. You're the best we've had in a long time. Now I'm back to stay."

"Well, I'm complimented that I'm such a hit around here, Dianna. I'm glad you're here to stay. At this point, where would you rate yourself on a scale from one to five? One being the worst possible Catholic; five being the best?"

"Around a two I'd say," blushed Dianna.

"Do you have any suggestions how you might move up the scale? Since you are going to come to mass every week now, I'd inch you up a three."

"How about three and one-half if I register?"

"You've got a deal! Between now and your marriage date, what number would you want to arrive at? We do have a full six months."

"A four would be great, I guess. Maybe if I get to confession, make all those interesting classes on the Catholic faith you offer, and bake something for the Parish Festival, I could get there. But a five would be out of my league."

"It's out of my league, too, Dianna."
Rex looks up nervously about this time and grumbles, "What classes?"

"Rex, don't sweat it. We offer a six-week refresher course on the meaning of being Catholic. It's really for Dianna's sake. She deserves to have an adult understanding of her faith. But I would like you to accompany her so that you have more knowledge of the Catholic beliefs and values that shaped her. I guarantee we are not recruiting you."

"But what about the 'promise' I'm suppose to make in writing?"

"Rex, only the Catholic party gives his or her

word to do their best to baptize and raise the children in the faith, while being respectful of your conscience. Can you live with that?"

"Yes, as long as I'm not pushed into anything."

"I promise, but Dianna claims you to have an interest in joining our church down the road. Is she wrong?"

"No, she's right. Okay, I'll level with you. My parents raised me as a strict Lutheran. I memorized Bible verses, attended Sunday school and know the Lutheran Catechism backwards and forwards. I am surprised about how little Dianna knows about the Bible, and when I do have questions for her, she shrugs her shoulders. I think it would be good for her to get a 'refresher course', as you put it."

"Tell, me Rex, would you like your minister to preside at the wedding with me? If it means something to your family and you, I'm very open to your minister's active participation in the ceremony. We wouldn't celebrate your wedding during the mass, though, because that symbolizes complete unity—and we're not there yet. But he can help with the Bible readings, the homily and other parts of the ritual."

"Father, that is sure different than my grandfather says it used to be."

"You're right, Rex. We are now more open, since our society is so pluralistic. If it was an extremely sensitive issue for you, permission could've been granted for the ceremony to take place at your Lutheran Church with or without me. That's how willing we are to accommodate.'

Dianna chimed in, "Father, there could be some problems in a mixed marriage, right? Tell us about them."

"Yes, Dianna, let me mention some common problems that could arise. A single parent, taking the child to church and sacramental preparation sessions later, could lead a very *lonely* life. The children could be torn about where to go and why the other parent doesn't share in the child's special celebrations."

"As you have heard, Dianna, this parish is more than a truck stop. We are developing a family focus, forming active support groups for young couples, organizing many social events; we are coming alive. If you are at all in touch with the rhythm of this church, you'll want the whole family to be involved. the children, again, will always wonder why Daddy can't share in this."

"This won't be an issue for us," interjected Rex, "since I'm warming up to the Catholic Church already. But I don't want to lose my heritage."

"Rex, don't let go of your heritage; if and when you enter the Catholic community, *share* your strengths with us: your emphasis on a personal relationship with Jesus, your love of the Bible, your experience of Christian fellowship groups...all these qualities will enhance the Catholic faith."

Unity in Diversity

Listen in on a different conversation now, between Gavin and Kristie. Gavin is a convinced and involved Catholic; his wife, Kristie, is equally involved in the local Baptist Church. Even as they were dating, their conversation often turned to faith issues and children. They were married in the Baptist Church, with the blessing of the Catholic community (a dispensation is sought), but Kristie will not compromise what she believes are important differences in the two traditions. She has agreed to have the children baptized and reared as Catholic but will not attend mass with them. She will worship in her Protestant community.

"Father," Gavin explained, "we have a workable, although difficult situation. My wife has major disagreements with some teachings of our church, and no amount of talking over the years has changed her position. I am uncomfortable with some of her fundamentalist doctrines as well. We decided to look for what we *can* share together."

"And what is that?"

"We always pray as a family at home: before meals, at bed time; and we have a special prayer service for twenty minutes each Sunday before dinner, where we intercede for personal intentions. We say these prayers from the heart, in our own words. The Bible is enthroned in a special corner of our house, and we discuss our life in Jesus freely with each other."

"Do you work as a family in any Christian Service projects?"

"Oh yes," replied Kristie, "we have adopted an older lady from the nursing home and spend time as a family with her each week. We also have a 'free will' bucket where extra coins are thrown in by each of us, then counted each month, and then put to a vote which charity it will go to."

"So, you maximize your time together, emphasizing your discipleship rather than your denomination with the children?"

"Yes, but they still wonder why I, the non-Catholic, don't come to mass with them. I then tell them that their Dad and I love Jesus, but sometimes we need to show it differently, much like we love them together, yet have special rituals with each, apart from the rest. We also tell them that we pray that one day the differences between our two Christian families will be gone—that's what Jesus wants—but we point out how good it is that we respect each other's traditions. We believe we are good role models in a society that doesn't always show us how to live in peace together."

I pray that my readers see the challenges of mixed marriages and openly discuss them. I hope that you learn as much about the other's faith as your research will take you. If there are values that point to head-on collisions in the future, it is important to face that *now* and make choices. It is better to be *one*, that is my bias! But, as illustrated by this second couple, a mixed marriage offers many creative opportunities to grow and share if you take them!

DISCUSSION QUESTIONS

1. Do we have religious differences that hold potential conflict?

2. Do I have any unanswered questions about my partner's religious traditions?

3. How will we create respect for both of our religions when it comes to raising our children?

11

Aging and Death

At age forty, the reality of how relative and subjective "growing old" can be, hit me in the face on a Hawaiian beach. Enjoying my vacation with my friends on one of the islands, I decided to take a refreshing plunge in the ocean at the stroke of midnight, to celebrate my birthday. Coming out of the water, I felt a surge of life, like I had tapped into the Fountain of Youth. My indomitable zest propelled me into a race down the beach, ready to kick sand in the face of any wimp who gawked.

Then my showdown came. Four teenage boys, with surfboards, shoved me out of their path, shouting, "Out of my way, old man." Until that moment, I felt rejuvenated, young. Then I realized that age is often in the eyes of the beholder.

Our society doesn't relish aging. Check the T.V. commercials, the billboards, the ads in magazines. If you want to be a little risqué, sneak a peak at the afternoon soaps and catch an eyeful of youth. These couples who light up your screen generate enough heat to kill aging cells. Have you noticed? Few are married, and those who succumbed fool around with their best friend's spouse.

We fear growing old because we fear dying—the other taboo. This is the last chapter because it is the last thing couples think about—at first.

Since we keep aging and death out of consciousness,

the shock of knowing a young man or woman who dies in an accident or of a fatal illness, leaving their spouse, traumatizes us. I have buried many young people, and seeing dreams perish before the bud blossoms hurts.

In this chapter, I will share the wisdom of a couple who has lived a long married life and end with their perspective on death.

It's Not Over Until It's Over

The aches and pains come more frequently, the hearing and sight diminish, but the flame doesn't have to die—so I'm told.

Claude and Maria have been stoking the fire for fifty years. Eavesdrop with me as they talk about their upcoming anniversary.

"Maria, fifty years gone by. Six children. Twenty-four grandchildren. Any regrets?"

"Sure, knowing what we know now, a few different decisions would've been made. But the best choice I ever made was marrying you."

"You know, Maria, I was thinking that this is a good time to be married and together. You've changed, though, you know."

"How have I changed?"

"Well, over the years you moved from quiet dependence to spunky independence. You seem to have opinions about everything these days and are not afraid to voice them. There was a time when raising the kids, taking care of the house *and* me was your whole life. Now you talk politics, argue with the pastor and let the kids fight their own battles. I've always loved you, but now I love you more. You're mighty interesting these days."

"Claude, you say I've changed. Do you know how you've mellowed? In those early years your days and nights were tied up in work. You wanted to be a good provider and you were! Sometimes you were so tired, after working two jobs, that you almost feel asleep at the dinner table. The kids didn't see much of you then, and neither did I. I admit, I was scared when the kids left and you retired. You had no hobbies and, without the kids around, I didn't know if we would have much to talk about. But we adjusted. You got into the garden, even got domestic. And the grandkids! You don't miss one of their games, and they know they can listen to your stories for hours. You're fun to be with, do you know that?"

"Fun? Sometimes you must feel like George Bush, saying 'Read my lips.' I can't hear as well and that frustrates me! I used to be able to do the chores, the "fix-it" list around the house. But no more. Since my heart attack, it's easy-does-it with everything. And that frustrates me, too. You are right about the workaholic I was in those early years. Truthfully, at times I feel useless, and I so want to buy you the things you always deserved. But with my limited income, I feel I've let you down." "The income might be limited, and our strength might be fading, but we've got some special things going for us at this time in our life that I value as a gift from God."

"Encourage me."

"Okay. First of all, we stop to smell the roses. We didn't use to; we'd step over them. It's safe to say that we're in no rush to go anywhere, and we don't let anybody rush us anymore. You don't have to be all business and I don't have to be all domestic. You learned how to share and I learned how to assert. We are *now* a team! And as far as money, we have enough. We are learning to live as the Lord asked us to live—simply."

"Maria, we are closer to the Lord, you're right. When we were young, appearances mattered more. We seem to have a clearer perspective on what matters in life today. It's the little things that excite us now: a walk together in the evening, attending daily mass (something we couldn't do when the kids were little), working *together* in the garden, shopping *together* on the weekends, talking *together* uninterrupted."

"Claude, look at how we're different from other couples our age who sit around like couch potatoes or become bingo junkies. We are foster grand-parents at the local school, working with the little ones who need special attention. You volunteer for meals-on-wheels for the homebound. I serve on the Parish Council as representative for senior citizens and, like you say, tell it like it is. We both attend a Bible study and are learning more at this age about our faith than we could ever have imagined. It's an exciting time for us as Catholics."

"Maria, I dread the thought of you dying someday. I don't know if I can go on without you. I hope I'm the first to go."

"Claude, I also think of our parting in death. That's when my faith in the Lord takes hold. As disciples of Jesus, we believe that death is not the final word, *life* is; love is not a fleeting thing; love is forever. We will always be together in Christ. *Always*."

"Maria, tomorrow we renew our wedding vows, celebrating fifty years of marriage. We have loved each other with the good and the bad, we have fought the good fight, and we will finish the race.

Let's thank God tomorrow for all the special graces he gave us, whatever form they took."

"And remember, my sexy husband, the best is yet to be. It's not over until it's over. Give me a kiss and say good night."

DISCUSSION QUESTIONS

1. In my "golden years" what do I hope to have accomplished?

2. What will my life be like without my partner? How will I go on?